Writing Wrongs: The Writing to Heal Workshop

About the course and workbook

This course is a systematic approach to thinking through and effectively dealing with trauma by using your own hands and thoughts. It takes time, it can be painful, and at times you may want to give up; but don't. Your discoveries and revelations will be worth it.

This course is designed such that a person will be able to follow it alone, within a group, or in a class setting. The group or class setting is preferred and encouraged for the initial cycle because there is built in peer support.

This workbook is written from a christian point of view and cites biblical references. These references contain wisdom - however this material should not be limited to just Christians and can be used for interfaith dialogue as well as with the greater community.

If you are a believer great! Welcome to this course. If you are not a believer, do not be turned off by the use of scripture or faith dialogue in this workbook. These positive statements and affirmations will still be of use to you. I welcome you to sit at the table with us, I welcome you to share, most of all I welcome you to be healed and get free.

Copyright 2016 Sheri Purpose Hall
Kansas City, MO
1 1 2 3 5 8 13

Table of Contents

Introduction	3
What is the healing process	4
How is recovery defined?	7
No Judgement Zone	8
The beginning FESTIVUS - Airing of grievances	9
Grievance and Feelings Charting Exercise - optional exercise	11
Post writing rules and prayer.	13
Cuss Words	14
Filthy Free Write	16
Post writing rules and prayer.	16
Dealing with What happened	17
What Happened? Just The Facts.	18
What Happened? Just The Feelings.	19
Post writing rules and prayer.	20
Anger	21
Angry Free Write	23
Post writing rules and prayer.	26
Guilt and Shame	27
What have I become - the result of trauma - do I love me?	27
Criminal Remorse writing	28
Post writing rules and prayer.	30
Apologies	31
Apologizing to others	32
Apologizing to myself	33
Post writing rules and prayer	34
Forgiveness	35
Forgiveness Exercises	37
Post writing rules and prayer.	39
The build up	41
Who am I now	44
Who can I be:	43
Affirmations:	44
Post writing rules and prayer.	45
Repeat!	46
Word Bank	47
Citations	54

Introduction

In life we have all suffered some sort of loss, regret, grief, or abuse. We have made bad decisions that led to other bad circumstances. We have been the innocent that was taken advantage of, and the one that was the perpetrator of harm. We have even had occasion to violate others as well as ourselves. Through all of this we have survived; and the fact that we are still here today tells the world that we are survivors. However, that survival does not come without a packed bag of resentment, unforgiveness, anger, guilt, and psychological trauma. Though we walk through this world with the face of conquerors, the reality of brokenness shines through. It oozes out of our communications, our actions, our strained relationships, our insecurities, etc. Trust me when I tell you what the rest of the world possibly has not. You're not hiding from anyone - we see you!.
We know you lie every time someone asks the question "How are you?" to wit you reply "Fine." with a smile. We know.

TIME OUT FOR THE LIES! TIME TO GET REAL! TIME TO HEAL!

I invite you to learn how to unpack some of this through the tool of writing. I promise this course will be as fun as it is reflective and serious. This course is put together so that all participants will walk away equipped with skills to systematically approach the healing process. And even if you do not choose to write another day in your life, you will at least be able to think, meditate, and pray, your way through the process.

I will not promise complete revelation because to promise such things would be a lie. You may receive revelation and freedom from certain things, other things you may need to continue to unpack. What I will promise is that you will become aware of the work and the road ahead towards mental and spiritual health.

This is not a one time wham bam course but something that could lead to (if you are willing to put in the work) a lasting positive change.

Always remember survivors, when you walked out of the situation, when the abuse stopped, when you survived WHATEVER you survived, that was only the beginning of the process. Survival does not equal healed.

What is the healing process

Adapted from Psychology Today Article - Recovering from Trauma

Not everyone who endures a traumatic experience is scarred by it; the human psyche has a tremendous capacity for recovery and even growth. Recovering from a traumatic experience requires that the painful emotions be thoroughly processed. Trauma feelings can not be repressed or forgotten. If they are not dealt with directly, the distressing feelings and troubling events replay over and over in the course of a lifetime, creating a condition known as post-traumatic stress disorder.

Whatever inner resources people need to mobilize for recovery, they still can not accomplish the task alone. Depression and trauma are disconnective disorders. They do not improve in isolation. To fix them you have to be connected to others.

Direct experience with disasters ranging from war and terrorism to hurricanes and earthquakes has taught me that there are four basic stages in recovering from a profound stress. Progression through all four stages is essential to recovery.

Stage One: Circuit-breaking

If you overload an electrical system with too much energy and too much stimulation, the circuit breaker activates and shuts everything down. The human nervous system is also an electrical system, and when it is overloaded with too much stimulation and too much danger, as in trauma, it also shuts down to just basics. People describe it as feeling numb, in shock or dead inside.

The juice turns off. Intellectually, you lose from 50 to 90 percent of brain capacity, which is why you should never make a decision when you're "in the trauma zone." Emotionally you don't feel anything. Spiritually you're disconnected, you have a spiritual crisis or it doesn't mean anything to you at all.

Physically all your systems shut down and you run on basics. What is so intriguing is that physical symptoms that were previously prominent often disappear during this time. Back pain, migraines, arthritis, even acne often clear up. Then, when recovery from trauma is complete, the physical symptoms return.

When the system starts to recover and can handle a bit more stimulation and energy—and the human system is destined to try to recover, to seek equilibrium—feelings begin to return.

Stage Two: Return of Feelings

Most people have not experienced so much primary trauma that they must see a professional counselor; they can work through their feelings by involving the people they are close to. They do it by telling their story—a hundred times. They need to talk talk talk, recount the gory details. That is the means by which they begin to dispel the feelings of distress attached to their memories.

The more that feelings can be encouraged, the better. The more you feel the more you heal.

The expression of feelings can take many forms. For most people it may be easiest to talk. But others may need to write. Or draw. However they tell their stories, the rest of us have an obligation to listen.

It is often helpful to actually revisit the scene of destruction. That allows someone who has been impacted directly to emotionally experience the event and grasp the reality of it. That direct experience can stimulate the return of feeling. Visiting the site is not for everybody, however. For some it is too disturbing. Others may need the support of loved ones to revisit the scene.

There are four broad patterns of expression of feelings that people employ in response to a crisis. Call them feeling styles. Some people consistently maintain one style; others exhibit all four styles at different times.

It is important to recognize which style of emotional expression is characteristic of your response, and which patterns your loved ones display. Each one demands a different approach.

The Trickle Effect

Feelings flow in little trickles, slow but steady. Tricklers have feelings at a low or medium level most of the time.

Hit and Run Feelings

Some people hit an emotion, experience it intensely, then find it so scary they run away from it. They avoid it and may not talk about it for days, weeks or even months. Then they hit the feeling again, it blows up and they run away from it again.

Roller Coasters

Many people go up and down emotionally. They are in touch with their feelings but their feelings are all over the place. Like a roller coaster, however, they can go very quickly through the feeling stage.

Tsunamis

Emotions come in tidal waves that are so big, comprehensive and overwhelming that those who get them feel like they're going to drown. They flail about, and then the wave recedes; they discover that they're still alive and they feel better. Tsunamis usually occur because people repress their feelings of pain.

Stage Three: Constructive Action

People need to take action and make a difference even in the smallest ways. Taking action restores a sense of control and directly counteracts the sense of powerlessness that is the identifying mark of trauma.

The ways of action are many. You can write a letter to the rescue workers. You can give blood. You can make a card for those who lost loved ones. You can hang a flag if that means something to you, or donate to the Red Cross. You can feed rescue workers or collect needed supplies for them from your community. You can take in children whose families can't reach them. You can help a person who is out of control to get more grounded during the crisis.

You do whatever you can and never assume that any gesture is too small. In a situation that is overwhelming, you don't go for the big picture. You go for what is closest to you and where you can make a difference. Constructive action might be writing about the catastrophe or creating some work of art about it. It also encompasses getting back to work so that you can contribute something.

Stage Two and Stage Three go hand in hand. To go forward you feel and you act. You can't do one or the other. Acting and feeling become an engine that propels you forward.

Stage Four: Reintegration

In the wake of crisis it is possible to learn and grow at rates 100 times faster than at any other time, because there is a door of opportunity. Growth can go at warp speed in every domain of life.

You can learn much that is deep and profound. You do this by interacting and by working together on the meaning of the difficult experience. Those who have the courage to become part of the trauma tribe, to experience and share their pain, or to help them overcome their pain, also have the opportunity to share their growth.

Everyone who goes through this process ends up better, stronger, smarter, deeper, and more connected. They would say so and everyone who comes in contact with them recognizes the change. It is like having a broken bone. If it heals properly, it is stronger in the spot where it fractured than it was before the injury.

Traumatic experiences are broken bones of the soul. If you engage in the process of recovery, you get stronger. If you don't, the bones remain porous, with permanent holes inside, and you are considerably weaker.

In this stage of recovery, you reintegrate yourself and your values in a new way. You incorporate meaning in your life. You integrate deeper and more authentic ways of communicating.

People at this stage may experience a new sense of the preciousness of life, a clarification of goals and renewed commitment to them, and new understanding of the value of ties to others. But to get to stage four you have to go through the first three stages.

How is recovery defined?

Recovery is the destruction of walls that would deter a person from realizing and speaking their truth. Recovery does not have an end, rather it is an ongoing cyclical process by which a community member pours out and the community pours in.

The four stages within the recovery cycle are:
1. Identifying the trauma. This is done either through the writing process, the performance process, or through listening to the stories of others.
2. Assessing the trauma. Once the trauma has been identified, then the community member can reflect on it and understand its depth by picking it apart one word at a time.
3. Communicating the trauma. This can be done either by writing it down, sharing with the group, or sharing words/writing with group members outside group sharing time.
4. Communicating victory. This is a dynamic point in the process. We often see a writer communicate trauma and victory all in the same piece of writing. This means that through the writing process they have been able to effectively use the outlet take the issue apart, and put themselves back together. And now we are here celebrate with them.

No Judgement Zone

"Who are me to judge?" Andrew Chad Caldwell

Yes, I did quote *him*. Some may not know who this man is and his entire history is not important. However, I present to you that he is simply an imperfect vessel that made a very good point using very bad grammar; but then again "Who are me to judge?". Rather than focusing on this crime against grammar, let us focus on the message. Who am I to judge ANYONE? We are all going through different traumas (This is the reason you are doing this correct?). What you may see as simple may be very complex to the next soul. Each and every one of us handle things differently. Therefore while going through this workshop unleash your inner empath. Make eye contact, hug, actively listen. This helps everyone in the group to feel safe and important.

This is a protected environment. What is said during this workshop stays within the workshop. With that being said - after you flip this page it is a judgement free zone!

As you can see, you have a small amount of space at the bottom of this page. That is ALL the room you have for judgment. If you just MUST pass judgement … write it here or forever hold your peace.

_____

_____

_____

_____

_____

_____

_____

"Judge not, that you be not judged. For with the judgment you pronounce you will be judged, and with the measure you use it will be measured to you. Why do you see the speck that is in your brother's eye, but do not notice the log that is in your own eye? Or how can you say to your brother, 'Let me take the speck out of your eye,' when there is the log in your own eye? You hypocrite, first take the log out of your own eye, and then you will see clearly to take the speck out of your brother's eye. …
Matthew 7:1-29 ESV

The beginning FESTIVUS - Airing of grievances

"It's festivus for the REST OF US!"
Character Frank Costanza - Seinfeld

The first step to healing is acknowledging the hurt is there. So you decide, you can continue with the tradition that most people have of suppressing and hurting or you can join us in a year round festivus!

During this process you will find many hurts, hurts that you had not previously thought of. You will begin to uncover more and more - don't shy away from this. Write as much as you can. As you go through this process you may think of more things - revisit this list and write them down.

Grievances and hurts:

_____

_____

_____

_____

_____

_____

_____

_____

_____

_____

_____

_____

_____

Grievance and Feelings Charting Exercise - optional exercise

Now that you have written your hurts it is time to chart the feelings behind those hurts. This will help you to more effectively get to the bottom of those hurts and find real solutions to situations.

Example:

Main issue: I HATE THE SUN

Feeling 1 - It's hot

    Digging 1 - I hate sweating

Feeling 2 - It's Bright

    Digging 1a - My head spins sometimes because of the heat.

    Digging 2 - I work outside

    Jackpot - I don't really hate the sun - I hate my job. I need a new job.

Feeling 3 - I have to deal with people during the day

    Digging 2a - I get very few breaks, and I feel unappreciated.

    Digging 3 - People always want something.

Feeling 4 - I work during the day

Grievance exercise

Main Issue _____

Post writing rules and prayer.

And you will know the truth, and the truth will set you free.
John 8:32 ESV

And let us not grow weary of doing good, for in due season we will reap, if we do not give up.
Galatians 6:9 ESV

After doing this exercise visit this list often, update it. We are humans in a human world, as we live people will continue to let us down, and just as often we let ourselves down. Write these things down. Checkmark those things that you have been able to heal from but never erase. This list doubles as a chart for your successes. Again, visit this page to see how far you've come and how far you have left to go. Remember, progress is the promise here, not completion or perfection.

Dear God,

The person starting this exercise is at the beginning of the healing process and will need you to help them complete it. I bind the enemy and all his forces as we know he comes to kill, steal, and destroy. Adversary you are on notice, you have no power here. You will not steal their peace or joy as a matter of fact you will relinquish everything you stole from them.

Lord, place your hand of protection on this endeavor as this person works toward mental, emotional, and spiritual freedom. Sweep the corners of their mind and heart to ensure that all hurts are accounted for. Please Lord, if they should cry during this process, hear their tears as prayers from your throne. If they grow weary, or frustrated, energize them Lord. Continue to bring fresh revelation through this process and make them whole.

In your name I pray,

Amen.

Cuss Words

"Cuss words just let em flow; mutha fuckin shit, got damned, asshole"
Cuss Words by Too $hort

Yes, you like to cuss. You love it. It has become common within our societies to express any feelings, anger *(Dammit!)*, rage and hurt *(Fuck you!)*, frustration *(Shit!)*, happiness, even excited agreement *(Yes Bitch!)* with a cuss word. And even if you do not say the words aloud - you find them creeping into your mental processes. That is fine - God gives us the renewal of our minds daily. However - out of the abundance of the heart the mouth speaks. Some of the subjects you will deal with while on this path will bring you to a place where you either have no words to say or you have nothing nice to say at all.

However, I recognize that all things are lawful to us, but they are not all expedient *1 Corinthians 6:12*. Do not be mastered by these words, bring them under control. Though it may feel good to let em flow, it may not be expedient to your health in the long run as you have neglected the true feelings behind the obscenity. The truth is some of the things that we have been through are worse than the words we use to express our feelings about them, the cuss words turn to curses as they force us to remain in a box not having truly released what we feel. We have not communicated effectively.

Now I know - that there will be people that read this thinking "I'm still gonna cuss." Cool - this is a no judgement zone. However, I would be remiss if I did not make you aware of the potential harm to yourself

These words have become containers of easy accessibility making the way that we use language lazy. Many people can hardly express a feeling without the use of one of these words. So in essence you are trapped. What happens when someone at your place of employment or at your place of worship angers you? There are 2 ways this could go. Either you will spew word vomit all over the situation, burning bridges and possibly disrespecting everyone within earshot. Or you will reluctantly restrain yourself, leaving all of the feelings inside and the offense will continue to occur. Without the adequate use of language you are disarmed. You may be able to fight, but not in the right way.

However, we cannot deny that spewing a full battery of vulgarity over a situation is not both awe inspiring and sometimes a much needed release.

So, this exercise will be a "Filthy Free Write". Say all the things that you always wanted to say, LET IT RIP! Make it dirty, nasty, horrid, reprehensible, just write and write and write and write until your heart's content!

Filthy Free Write

LET IT RIP!

Post writing rules and prayer.

I tell you, on the day of judgment people will give account for every careless word they speak,
Matthew 12:36 ESV

Let your speech always be gracious, seasoned with salt, so that you may know how you ought to answer each person.
Colossians 4:6 ESV

Did it feel good even wonderful perhaps to "get that off". I'm glad for you, elated even! But here's the catch (I'm sure you knew there was one coming.), going forward your access to all those cuss words in your goody bag is limited. The only allowable cuss words are direct quotations of what another person said to you, about you, or about your loved ones. They must reference a specific situation but not necessarily your feelings towards it. Unless it is absolutely unavoidable, please refrain from all cuss words. Remember in the beginning of this exercise I described those words as "empty containers"? This will do you no good if you are not able to accurately describe your feelings. If you cannot think of any other way, ask for a word, use the thesaurus, or use the word bank. By the end of this workbook you will be fully equipped with tools and resources to use your words effectively.

Note: If you have a problem doing this, you can always use the Shakespearean Insult Kit located within the word bank. Not only are these NOT 4/5 letter swear words; you might find them more effective, descriptive, and downright funny than your "regular" insults.

Dear God,

Help the person pressing on through this healing to really dig deep and find the right way to communicate their trauma. It is hard to be descriptive when your feelings are hurt, when you are scared, when you are tired, when your patience is tried, or when a crime has been committed against you. It is hard to really reflect and understand how torn and broken you are. Lord help us to walk forward bravely, you created us as conquerors. You have NOT given us the spirit of fear, but of power, love, and a sound mind. We are not powerless against the words that come out of our mouths, we will learn to love ourselves and heal through this. You have given us a sound mind so that we can process all of this. Thank you Lord for this!.

In your name we pray,

Amen

Dealing with What happened

"And so I cry sometimes when I'm lying in bed
Just to get it all out, what's in my head
And I, I am feeling a little peculiar"
What's Going On by 4 Non Blondes

Revisit that list of grievances. Choose one that you want to deal with right now. Choose wisely.

Got it?

Good. Let's break this down.

The first thing we are going to do is to deal with what happened. There is no flowery language or inspiration for this part. This is where you tell it like it is. However, there is a method to this.

In order to ensure that you will gain the maximum benefit from this process, you want to make sure that this is a trauma you can go the distance with. To do this we will write the happenstance 2 ways. First we will just write the facts, no feelings, no frills. Next we will just write feelings. This is also a teeter - totter process in that as you reveal the feelings you will think of more details regarding the situation.

Number the facts as you write them. When you write the feelings make them correspond to a fact. You can make each part as long or as short as i needs to be to adequately explain what happened and your feelings behind it. After you have written all of the corresponding feelings/facts entries make one more entry in the feelings section. These feelings do not have to correspond to the facts but can correspond to the whole situation, your overall emotion, etc.

Example:

Facts:

1. He spoke to me in a loud tone.
2. He pushed me.
3. I fell.

Feelings
1. I felt threatened.
2. I was confused, I didn't quite understand what was going on. It all happened very quickly.
3. When I hit the ground I felt disgusted. I couldn't believe that someone I loved did this. I felt betrayed.
4. He used to make me feel safe, now I don't know what to expect. At first I thought that it would stop but it just kept going like a train wreck.

What Happened? Just The Facts.

What Happened? Just The Feelings.

Post writing rules and prayer.

For I know the plans I have for you, declares the Lord, plans for welfare and not for evil, to give you a future and a hope. Then you will call upon me and come and pray to me, and I will hear you. You will seek me and find me, when you seek me with all your heart.
Jeremiah 29:11-13 ESV

While working through this you may find that you are able to rectify the issue within yourself right here. In that sense, this exercise can also be used as a stand-alone exercise to help "sort out" smaller issues and deal with them accordingly. Sorting the actual events of what happened from the feelings helps to give us a clearer view of the situation in its entirety. This exercise helps with both self validation and "realism". After this exercise, review what you wrote. Come to terms with the facts. Be "real" with yourself in evaluating your feelings:

1. Did this really happen the way I thought it did?
2. Was I in physical danger or was I physically harmed?.
3. Was I emotionally harmed?
4. Did I react based on this situation or other similar situations?
5. Did I take this the wrong way.
6. Was I overreacting?
7. Why have I not been able to move past this?
8. Am I really hurt by this or is my ego just bruised.
9. Was this really important. (relationship and offense are important factors in determining importance.)
10. On a scale of 1-10 how serious was this. (Take into account the previous questions. Also importance is not the same as seriousness. A person could commit a moderately serious offense, but it may not be as important because there is no established relationship with the person.)

Take time to write down your answers to the questions of importance and seriousness. This will help you to deal with issues in a real way. By asking and answering these questions about the situation you may be able to immediately forgive a close acquaintance or you may need to dig for deeper healing with an entirely different issue.

Dear God,

Pull the covers off! Reveal the truth to us through this exercise. Allow us to get an up close and personal look at the situation and the pain. Help us Lord! Help us to see with new eyes and clear vision so that we can put things into proper perspective. We know that you are all powerful and are able to help us in this. We cannot do this without you. Thank you for your faithfulness in this and in every situation

In your name we pray

Amen

Anger

"I HATE YOU SO MUCH RIGHT NOW!"
I Hate you so much right now by Kelis

What is anger?

"Anger is an emotion characterized by antagonism toward someone or something you feel has deliberately done you wrong. Anger can be a good thing. It can give you a way to express negative feelings, for example, or motivate you to find solutions to problems. But excessive anger can cause problems. Increased blood pressure and other physical changes associated with anger make it difficult to think straight and harm your physical and mental health."

Adapted from the Encyclopedia of Psychology

Yes ANGER, one of my favorite and most loathed emotions. People love to be angry. They say "I'm gonna tell it like it is." (Until fear sets in and clamps down on your larynx disabling your ability to speak.) They look at people from across the room with disgust in their eyes lying in wait to pounce. (Until the person they were waiting to pounce on gives them the WARMEST greeting of their lives and they don't quite know how to react.) That is the thing about anger, dealing with it can be confusing at times because humans are unpredictable creatures. The same way you may have been planning a confrontation is the same way the person you were planning on confronting was either not thinking about you or planning an escape from aforementioned confrontation.

Physiologically anger causes your teeth to clinch, temperature and blood pressure to raise, body stiffens, eyes strain, teeth clench, jaw becomes rigid, breathing deepens, skin may change colors, neck and muscles contort etc. WOW! That sounds like the Incredible Hulk. If you recall the way that he looks when he goes "hulk", he looks like he is on the verge of combustion. That seems VERY stressful.

There is anger that causes this type of response. This is the type of anger that not only arises upon a violation, but arises every time you think about a certain situation, see a certain person, think of that person, or revisit a certain place. It is memory driven anger. This is a tool of the enemy that works to destroy your very being. Soon you find yourself dwelling on that person, situation, or place, and all of the same physiological effects come back again stronger because now you have remembered more parts of the issue that possibly should have angered you at that time. Then you begin to be angry at yourself. Why didn't I see this coming. Why didn't I stop this. Why didn't I tell someone sooner. Why did I allow _____. Why didn't I _____. (Fill in your blanks accordingly.)

Yes. Anger is okay for a little while but staying like that as it works to our benefit. However, walking around with all of that on you like a ticking time bomb certainly is not healthy and must be dealt with in a healthy way.

In our anger exercise we are going to work this out!

Externally Directed Anger

First we are going to address our externally directed anger. Externally directed anger is just as it sounds, anger directed towards anyone or anything external. During this exercise you will write everything about the situation, the people involved (or the people who were not there that you feel should have been) that makes you angry. Go back to that place, that time, those people and write (revisit the "Just the Facts" exercise for assistance here). Write ANGRILY. Write non-sense, gibberish. Don't be afraid to bumble through the words. But remember to USE WORDS - if you need more words, visit the word bank in the back of the book.

After the initial "spew". Then write the names of the people that you are specifically angered with. Write why you are angry with them. Then then write why you are holding on to the anger for them.

Internally Directed Anger

Next, internally directed anger. Why are you angry at yourself? What could you have done? What did you do? Again - Write ANGRILY. Write non-sense, gibberish. Don't be afraid to bumble through the words. But remember to USE WORDS - if you need more words, visit the word bank in the back of the book.

Responsibility Assignment

Yes, we assigning fault, we are placing blame. Yes. Often placing blame and assigning fault are discouraged but let's be honest, if we are to be held accountable, someone must be responsible. Someone is responsible for your hurt, for your trauma, for your suffering, and for your pain. Normally it is not just one person. Could someone have protected you better? Could you have protected you better? Could the police have shown up faster? Did the community breed the monster? Is the establishment to blame? The list could get wrong when connecting the dots of why things happen the way they happen and why people are the way they are.

If during these exercises you feel yourself going to a place you do not want to be, STOP. Take a break. Think, talk, pray, consult your community. Also, in the word bank there is a Shakespearean Insult Kit. Use it for a little humor. Look at the name of the person that angered you, envision their face and hurl shakespearean insults at them until your belly fills with laughter. Laughter from a healthy place is the BEST medicine and the Best gift you can give yourself.

Angry Free Write

Directed:

Internal:

Responsibility Assignment:

Post writing rules and prayer.

Beloved, never avenge yourselves, but leave it to the wrath of God, for it is written, "Vengeance is mine, I will repay, says the Lord."
Romans 12:19 ESV

It is okay to have anger.
It is permissible.
Sometimes it is necessary.

Allow yourself to be angry, you deserve it, you are human. But do not find a resting place in anger. Anger is a bubbling pot that has a tendency to boil over into other things, bitterness, jealousy, pride, greed (yes pride and greed can be fed by anger). Anger is a valid emotion that if dealt with is effective. However if not resolved can be damaging. The point of this exercise was to pinpoint your areas of anger. Lay them all out in front of you so that you have a visual representation of all that is inside of you. Now that it is out, let us move forward. I know the weight isn't lifted just yet - we are still on an exploratory mission, but be patient. We are getting there.

Dear God,

You know who we are deep down on the inside. You know our hurts, our pains, our scars. You know the furnace deep within that burns hot with fury. You made us in your image so you know our wrath and our indignation, righteous or otherwise. Lord help us to get to the root, the core, the bottom of what stokes these fires, help us to quench them with more of you. Please help us to continue on this journey so that we can be healed.

In your name,

Amen.

Guilt and Shame

"Loving you is complicated, loving you is complicated"
"I can feel your vibe and recognize that you're ashamed of me
Yes, I hate you, too"
U by Kendrick Lamar

What have I become - the result of trauma - do I love me?

Analyzing this is tough. I get it. But working it through will be worth it. I am sure at this point you are mentally and spiritually exhausted. I get that too. However this is normally where these filthy, icky feelings set in. Guilt and shame are kindred however they are different.

Guilt:

This is the part where you feel bad about something that you have done. In the previous exercise we did a "responsibility assignment" so that you could clearly see what is your fault and what is not your fault. During that exercise you may have realized that you have feelings towards things that were outside of your control. However, also during that exercise you may realize that you have feelings towards some things that are within your control. That is healthy. That is honest guilt. That is you looking in the mirror and taking responsibility for where you messed up. Guilt is an emotion that aids in holding us accountable to ourselves when correctly applied.

Shame:

This is the part where you feel bad about yourself. WHOA - not healthy. You are not a horrible person, you are not what *THEY* said you were no matter what happened or what you did there is still redemption. Continuing to hold on to shame does you no benefit. "Beating up on" yourself continuously has no added benefit. "Beating up on" yourself continuously for the benefit of onlookers only aids them in not moving past the situation, it stunts growth; and at a certain point it begins to look contrived. As long as you continue to hold on others will have a hard time healing as well. Guilt is one thing, it is honest. Shaming oneself or allowing yourself to be shamed is harmful.

It doesn't matter if you stole a penny candy or if you are a child molester *(yikes!)* as much as society hates to admit it (myself included) you cannot shame yourself and expect to live. Do the work, look at your actions, examine yourself, find out why you did what you did, so that you can make the necessary repairs and never repeat it. Sure, depending on the offense there are going to be people that will forever hate you. There are people that your very existence offends and you didn't have to anything but be born! They are not the focus right now, you are. Your health is important enough to take center stage here. If one component of our community is unhealthy it can start a chain reaction that leads to more trauma, more hurt, more actions that cannot be undone. So your health is not only important to you, but it is also important to me, your loved ones, and the people in the community abroad.

Remember: A healthy you has so much more to offer than the you that is stuck on hating you.

Criminal Remorse writing

What do you feel guilty about?
Write it down.
Then analyze it.
Are these things really your fault?

If they are, write down solutions for these issues. Write ways that you can make sure they never happen again. Then write ways that you can make sure others don't follow down the same path.

If they are NOT. Put one line through each item that was truly out of your control. DO NOT ERASE. Examine these entries. Count up the cost. Some of us have been holding onto shame that never truly belonged to us. Keep this list as a visual reminder to be free of these things.

_____

_____

_____

_____

_____

_____

_____

_____

_____

_____

_____

_____

_____

_____

_____

_____

Post writing rules and prayer.

There is therefore now no condemnation for those who are in Christ Jesus.
Romans 8:1 ESV

Now that you have a clear cut listing of all these things - keep it, visit it often. Visit it when you doubt yourself and find your mind troubled. Visit it when those feelings of guilt creep back in. Know that you have a plan that can aid you in never making the same mistake again. Also know that you can help others to avoid the same pitfalls that you fell into. you are forgiven. You are useful. You are here for a purpose. You are not what happened to you. You are not what you did. You are human, a beautifully made representation of God; crafted in his image. You are the apple of His eye.

Never forget it.

Dear God,

GIVE THEM FREEDOM! Free the chains of guilt and shame. None of us are perfect, not one! Encourage them, help them find their self-worth in you. Lord, put them to work for you. Their experiences give them the necessary first hand knowledge to aid in the recovery of others. Give them their smiles back, restore their joy, rekindle their fire for you, and give them an abundance of peace. Allow them to find rest in you so that they are weighed down by this thing no more.

In your name,

Amen.

Apologies

Caleb - "I am sorry. I have been so selfish. For the past 7 years I have trampled on you with my words and with my actions. I have loved other things when I should have loved you. In last few weeks God has given me a love for you that I never had before. I have asked Him to forgive me;and I am hoping and praying that somehow you can forgive me too."
Catherine - "I just need some time to think."
Caleb - "You can have all the time you need."
Caleb and Catherine Holt in Fireproof.

As we are going through our traumas we (whether intentionally or unintentionally) hurt others. Who have you been while dealing with this? Have you not been the nicest person? Have you jumped to snap judgements of people? Have you treated someone unfairly or harshly? Did the person even know they had a hand in your hurt? Did you let them know? Did you give them a chance to make it right? Did you put unfair expectations on people? This list could go on and on.

An apology is an invitation for forgiveness. It is an open door. Open that door. You may say to yourself - why would a person need an invitation to forgive, they should be able to sort that out within themselves. This is true, but not always the case. The same could be said for the apology - what took you so long to process your wrongs. Realize throughout this process that you are dealing with humans. Through the hustle and bustle of life, some things take a back seat. Other things stay at the forefront and we just do not deal with them. This exercise is helping you to approach this head on. You get to take the reigns.

Take this time, this exercise to first write down the names of those that you want to apologize to.
Then write apologies. It doesn't have to be long. The quotation above has all the perfect elements of an unselfish apology.

1. Say the words - I am sorry or I apologize.
2. Admit your wrongs
3. Say how you came to this apology, what made you realize you were in the wrong.
4. Give the other person time to process the apology, everyone is not always quick with forgiveness. Sometimes, just like it took you time to apologize, it takes time for people to process the sincerity of your apology and actually verbalize forgiveness.

After you get through your list of people, turn the lens around. Apologize to yourself. Did you beat yourself up? Did you no offer yourself the proper treatment? Did you not think yourself worthy? Did you isolate yourself and stop doing things that you love? Apologize. Give the same focus and effort towards the apology to yourself and you did for everyone else.

Hurt people, hurt people, including themselves.

Apologizing to others

Apologizing to myself

Post writing rules and prayer

If possible, so far as it depends on you, live peaceably with all.
Romans 12:18 ESV

You did it! You have come so far. You should be proud of yourself. I am proud that you made it this far. It takes maturity to apologize, and it takes even more maturity to apologize to yourself. If you previously felt like you didn't love yourself, this is the first step on a long road to self love. Celebrate this. Pat yourself on the back. Apologizing for many people is hard. It is hard to admit when you have done wrong, even if you are only talking to yourself.

Now, the next step. All those people that you declared deserve apologies, give them to them. Why waste a good apology? You already wrote it. You already identified the issue(s). You are aware and capable. You can do this. I believe in you. Be brave. Face this head on.

You can.

I know.

Dear God,

Thank you. Thank you for progress. Thank you for the workings of a sound mind and spirit. You didn't have to bring us this far but you did and for that we thank you. You are awesome. In areas that are painful, you make people grow, blossom, and bloom. Now Lord, equip them for the road ahead. There is still much work to be done. However we cannot move forward without acknowledging the victories we have already had.

Thank you!

In your name we pray,

Amen.

Forgiveness

"I never ever wanna press rewind, never wanna go back in time
Not much glory in that story but it's mine
So I'm loving who I am today, past has passed away
Finally I have forgiven me"
Forgiven ME by Mary Mary

As I said in the previous exercise, an apology is an invitation for forgiveness. You invited yourself to forgive and be forgiven.

You gave yourself permission to forgive and be forgiven.

It's okay to forgive and be forgiven.

Do not continue to allow issues to live in your heart and mind, stirring up all these emotions. And I know, some things have layers. You think that you are over it, and you are down the rabbit hole again. You may say that "I have tried to forgive and failed." It's okay. We have all done this. So often we are taught to forgive, forgive, forgive, without actually sorting the matter out. As you have gone through these exercises, you have sorted the matter out. You have thought about it. You have thought about your position and role in it. You have thought about everyone else involved. You have swallowed the pill of humility and admitted where you were wrong and apologize. You have done the work.

So here we are, at more work to do. Yes, I know. You are tired. But all of the work that you have done has led up to this. Forgiveness.

Forgiveness must be done intentionally. It is not a passive thing, it is a revolutionary thing. Forgiveness breaks chains, and moves mountains. If you do not believe it - ask a person whose family was feuding over something foolish their whole lives what happens when one person opens an opportunity to forgive. Suddenly, the very thing that people thought could not be done has been done. The mountains between them crumble and the family becomes unified. That is the power of forgiveness. You have this power. You also have the wisdom, knowledge, and authority to carry it out.

Forgiveness doesn't mean that you will be in the same position that you were before you were violated. Forgiveness does not mean that you are no longer aware, or that you do not operate in wisdom. You must continue to exercise the muscle of discernment.

External Forgiveness:

Think on the people that you are going to forgive. From the smallest offense to the huge one, why should they receive forgiveness? If for nothing other than to relieve your spirit, you must forgive. I know, people have done some seemingly unforgivable things. I believe that you are powerful beyond what you can think, see or imagine. If this is true, forgiveness is not outside of your reach.

Internal Forgiveness

While you are forgiving all those other people, save some room for yourself. Forgive yourself. You apologized to yourself, now it is your chance to respond. Revisit those areas of shame and forgive yourself. Forgive yourself for thinking lowly of you. Forgive yourself for those times where you felt that you should have been able to protect yourself. Forgive.

You deserve to be forgiven.

You deserve to be free.

Do it now. Don't waste another minute.

Forgiveness Exercises

External Forgiveness:

Internal Forgiveness:

Post writing rules and prayer.

Blessed are the peacemakers, for they shall be called sons of God.
Matthew 5:9 ESV

Pay attention to yourselves! If your brother sins, rebuke him, and if he repents, forgive him,
Luke 17:3 ESV

YES! Congratulations. You are a peacemaker. You have made peace within yourself, you have made peace with others. You have made peace. This forgiveness was for you. You needed to free up some space in your heart. You need to free up some space in your mind. You needed to free up some space within your life. You needed this more than anyone else.

You completed an act of spiritual maturity. You can go forth and shout it to the mountains proudly and really mean it. I forgave!

However, there is a warning to this. Trauma has many levels. It can manifest itself in multiple areas. Just when you thought that you truly forgave and meant it this time, sometimes a picture, a sighting, or an occurrence can reopen the wound. DO NOT BE AFRAID. DO NOT DOUBT. This is normal and healthy. Though you thought that you made an exhaustive list of everything going through this process, there still may be areas that you have forgotten, areas that you have no totally dealt with, and areas that may need to be dealt with again because you are still sore there. Think of trauma as a wound. Some wounds are deeper than others, some are wider. That is okay. You have the capacity to forgive. Forgiveness takes time. Not just time passing from the original violation, but time for your brain to process. If the wound is still sore, go back and reread what you wrote concerning the subject, seek you peer support, and pray. Continue to work it out, bandaging the wound with a clean dressing until fully healed

For many of you, you have let these hurts sit for years! They have become infected! An infection takes time to heal. It takes the right amount of antibiotic. Luckily, now, you have been equipped with the medicine for it. Be patient with yourself here. Allow the healing to take its course.

Now I challenge you to use discernment. Go through that list of people that you forgave and figure out who needs to hear that you forgave them. We know that many people are not spiritually mature enough to accept forgiveness, especially when they feel they have done nothing wrong. Even when you are sincere, there are those that will look at you and behave as though you are trying to start trouble. "Oh the nerve of him to forgive ME." Steer clear of those ones unless you want to be angered or truly saddened by their lack of maturity.

There are people that you can have this conversation with that will really try to understand how you felt. They are beneficial, go to them. Verbally make peace with these people. You will be surprised at how caring and compassionate some can be. There are some that may say "I had no idea I hurt you like that, I apologize for that and I accept your forgiveness." There are others that may say "I knew I hurt you, thank you for coming to me because I really didn't know apologize for what I did." This moment of forgiveness doesn't mean that you have to invite them into your life and take up with them as if you never missed a beat. It simply means that you are free and you have allowed the other person to be free.

Dear God,

Forgiveness is hard, but I thank you for taking us through it. I thank you for giving it to us. IF we did not have the power to forgive we would be stuck in the past, spinning our wheels, trying to find a way out. We thank you for spiritual maturity and growth. We thank you for bringing us peace on so many levels. Thank you. Lord please increase our discernment, it is one of the defenses you gave us to help protect us. Help us to use discernment wisely rather than operating in fear and putting up needless walls. Keep your hand of protection upon us as we finish this journey.

In your name we pray,

Amen

The build up

Whew! You have been drained of all of this! This was work, time consuming! Luckily YOU'RE WORTH EVERY BIT OF IT! You are important enough for this to take the time that it did. You are special and loved. If you do not feel love from others, you have just completed a work of self love through this workbook and are going to continue that in this exercise.

It is important that you know your own importance, that you know you own worth.

You may have been told that you were worthless - that was a lie.
You may have been told that you were nothing - that was a lie.
You may have been told that you didn't matter - that was a lie.
You may have been told that no one loved you - that was a lie.
You may have been told that the world would be better off without you -that was a lie.
You may have been told that you were a mistake - that was a lie.
You may have been told that all you are good for is _____ (fill in the blank) - that was a lie.
You may have been told that you were a horrible person - that was a lie.
You may have felt that people just do what they want with you - no more.
You may have felt like the doormat on the entryway of abuse - no more.
You may have felt like a horrible human being - no more.
You may have felt like a good for nothing _____(fill in the blank) - no more.
You may have felt like you didn't even want to be here any more - no more.

It is time to fix all of this. Through this exercise you will build yourself up. You are going to come out of this process stronger than you came in.

First: Write who you are now. Take a good look at yourself, examine. Write down the good, the bad and the ugly.

Second: Write who you want to be. Now that you have identified areas of improvement figure out how you are going to get there. Visualize the person that you want to be, see yourself being that person. Write that down.

Third: Affirmations. On this journey to being who you want to be you will need encouragement along the way. Many people use daily affirmation statements, they say them in the mirror in the morning after they awake and they start their day with them. You will create your own affirmation statements. In the word bank you will find a list of positive words. You will also find a list of biblical affirmations. Look at these and create as many as you need to remind yourself who you are.

Who am I now

Who can I be:

Affirmations:

Post writing rules and prayer.

And we know that for those who love God all things work together for good, for those who are called according to his purpose.
Romans 8:28 ESV

But you, beloved, building yourselves up in your most holy faith and praying in the Holy Spirit, keep yourselves in the love of God, waiting for the mercy of our Lord Jesus Christ that leads to eternal life.
Jude 1:20-21 ESV

Remember who you are.

You just told yourself, you wrote it. Now say it. Say it aloud so that you can hear the sound of your voice, strong and able. You are who you say you are. You are who God says you are. You are.

Remember.

Never Forget.

Dear God,

Thank you for making us in your image. We are fearfully and wonderfully made, each of us different and useful right here. We are the atmosphere setters, the community changers, and the peacemakers. We can make a difference in ourselves and in those around us. Thank you for trusting us with such power. Thank you for giving us authority and dominion. Thank you for loving us. Thank you for helping us to love our neighbors, and thank you for helping us to love ourselves. Lord increase our faith in ourselves and in you as we continue to work through other hurts. Increase our patience. Increase yourself in us.

In your name we pray,

Amen.

Repeat!

Yes the finish line! BUT WAIT! This chapter is named REPEAT! Do you mean that after all of this you want me to repeat ... YES!

There are 3 types of people that make it through this workbook.

Type 1: That is way TOO much writing, never doing that again, but now that I have these tools, I can systematically think, pray, and talk my way through these things.

Type 2: This is great information paired with great exercises. I do not think that need to do the whole workbook over and over, but I think that I can use a few of the exercises to help me through.

Type 3: This is exactly what I needed! Onto the next situation I need to heal from.

I think it is great that you all got something out of this. I encourage you to use these exercises together so that you can completely work through a thing with knowledge and total understanding. This course is built such that you can use each of the exercises as stand alone assignments for yourself. However you get the maximum benefit of each of the separate exercises when they are used together. Uncovering and healing trauma is like carefully peeling the layers of an onion one by one without cutting them. This takes work, patience, and time spent on self-care. YOU NEED TIME FOR SELF CARE. DON'T SKIMP ON YOURSELF!

Start the process over again, with a different hurt or a different trauma. Maybe the hurt or trauma is too big to tackle all at once. I encourage you to break things down into bite sized portions.

Keep striving for wellness. Never Give up!

Word Bank

Emotions

A
acceptance
admiration
adoration
affection
afraid
agitation
agreeable
aggressive
aggravation
agony
alarm
alienation
amazement
amusement
angry
anguish
annoyance
anticipation
anxiety
apprehension
assertive
assured
astonishment
attachment
attraction
awe
B
beleaguered
bewitched
bitterness
bliss
blue
boredom
C
calculating
calm
capricious
caring
cautious
charmed

cheerful
closeness
compassion
complacent
compliant
composed
contempt
conceited
concerned
content
crabby
crazy
cross
cruel
D
defeated
defiance
delighted
dependence
depressed
desire
disappointment
disapproval
discontent
disenchanted
disgust
disillusioned
dislike
dismay
displeasure
dissatisfied
distraction
distress
disturbed
dread
E
eager
earnest
easy-going
ecstasy
ecstatic

elation
embarrassment
emotion
emotional
enamored
enchanted
enjoyment
enraged
enraptured
enthralled
enthusiasm
envious
envy
equanimity
euphoria
exasperation
excited
exhausted
extroverted
exuberant
F
fascinated
fatalistic
fear
fearful
ferocity
flummoxed
flustered
fondness
fright
frightened
frustration
furious
fury
G
generous
glad
gloating
gloomy
glum
greedy

grief
grim
grouchy
grumpy
guilt
H
happiness
happy
harried
homesick
hopeless
horror
hostility
humiliation
hurt
hysteria
I
infatuated
insecurity
insulted
interested
introverted
irritation
isolation
J
jaded
jealous
jittery
jolliness
jolly
joviality
jubilation
joy
K
keen
kind
kindhearted
kindly
L
laid back
lazy

like
liking
loathing
lonely
longing
loneliness
love
lulled
lust
M
mad
merry
misery
modesty
mortification
N
naughty
neediness
neglected
nervous
nirvana
O
open
optimism
ornery
outgoing
outrage
P
panic
passion
passive
peaceful
pensive
pessimism
pity
placid
pleased
pressed
pride
proud
pushy

Q
quarrelsome
queasy
querulous
quick-witted
quiet
quirky
R
rage
rapture
rejection
relief
relieved
remorse
repentance
resentment
resigned
revulsion
roused
S
sad
sarcastic
sardonic
satisfaction
scared
scorn
self-assured
self-congratulatory
self-satisfied
sentimentality
serenity
shame
shock
smug
sorrow
sorry
spellbound
spite
stingy
stoical
stressed

subdued
submission
suffering
surprise
sympathy
T
tenderness
tense
terror
threatening
thrill
timidity
torment
tranquil
triumphant
trust
U
uncomfortable
unhappiness
unhappy
upset
V
vain
vanity
venal
vengeful
vexed
vigilance
vivacious
W
wary
watchfulness
weariness
weary
woe
wonder
worried
wrathful
Z
zeal
zest

Shakespearean Insult Kit
Combine one word from each of the columns below, prefaced with "Thou":

Column 1	Column 2	Column 3
artless	base-court	apple-john
bawdy	bat-fowling	baggage
beslubbering	beef-witted	barnacle
botless	beetle-headed	bladder
churlish	boil-brained	boar-pig
cockerd	clapper-clawed	bugbear
clouted	clay-brained	bum-bailey
craven	common-kissing	canker-blossom
currish	crook-pated	clack-dish
dankish	dismal-dreaming	clotpole
dissembling	dizzy-eyed	coxcomb
droning	doghearted	codpiece
errant	dread-bolted	death-token
fawning	earth-vexing	dewberry
fobbing	elf-skinned	flap-dragon
froward	fat-kidneyed	flax-wench
frothy	fen-sucked	flirt-gill
gleeking	flap-mouthed	foot-licker
goatish	fly-bitten	fustilarian
gorbellied	folly-fallen	giglet
impertinent	fool-born	gudgeon
infectious	full-gorged	haggard
jarring	guts-griping	harpy
loggerhead	half-faced	hedge-pig
lumpish	hasty-witted	orn-beast
mammering	hedge-born	hugger-mugger
mangled	hell-hated	joithead
mewling	idle-headed	lewdster
paunchy	ill-breeding	lout
pribbling	ill-nurtured	magot-pie
puking	knotty-pated	malt-worm
puny	milk-livered	mammet
qualling	motley-minded	measle
rank	onion-eyed	minnow
reeky	plume-plucked	miscreant
roguish	pottle-deep	moldwarp
ruttis	pox-marked	mumble-news
saucy	reeling-ripe	nut-hook
speeny	rough-hewn	pigeon-egg
spongy	rude-growing	pignut
surly	rump-fed	putock

tottering
unmuzzled
vain
venomed
villainous
warped
wayward
weedy
yeasty
cullionly
fusty
caluminous
wimpled
burly-boned
bisbegotten
odiferous
poisonous
fishified

shard-borne
sheep-biting
spur-galled
swag-bellied
tardy-gaited
tickle-brained
toad-spotted
unchin-snouted
weather-bitten
whoreson
malmsey-nosed
rampalian
lily-livered
scurvy-valiant
brazen-faced
bunch-back'd
leadeen-footed
muddy-mettled
pigeon-liver'd

pumpion
ratsbane
scut
skainsmate
strumpet
varlot
vassal
whey-face
wagtail
knave
blind-worm
popinjay
scullian
jolt-head
malcontent
devil-monk
toad
rascal

Positive words

A
absolutely
adorable
accepted
acclaimed
accomplish
accomplishment
achievement
action
active
admire
adventure
affirmative
affluent
agree
agreeable
amazing
angelic
appealing
approve
aptitude
attractive

D
dazzling
delight
delightful
distinguished
divine
E
earnest
easy
ecstatic
effective
effervescent
efficient
effortless
electrifying
elegant
enchanting
encouraging
endorsed
energetic
energized
engaging

graceful
great
green
grin
growing
H
handsome
happy
harmonious
healing
healthy
hearty
heavenly
honest
honorable
honored
hug
I
idea
ideal
imaginative
imagine

meaningful
merit
meritorious
miraculous
motivating
moving
N
natural
nice
novel
now
nurturing
nutritious
O
okay
one
one-hundred percent
open
optimistic
P
paradise
perfect

rewarding
right
robust
S
safe
satisfactory
secure
seemly
simple
skilled
skillful
smile
soulful
sparkling
special
spirited
spiritual
stirring
stupendous
stunning
success
successful

W
wealthy
welcome
well
whole
wholesome
willing
wonderful
wondrous
worthy
wow
Y
yes
yummy
Z
zeal
zealous

awesome	enthusiastic	impressive	phenomenal	sunny
B	essential	independent	pleasurable	super
beaming	esteemed	innovate	plentiful	superb
beautiful	ethical	innovative	pleasant	supporting
believe	excellent	instant	poised	surprising
beneficial	exciting	instantaneous	polished	T
bliss	exquisite	instinctive	popular	terrific
bountiful	F	intuitive	positive	thorough
bounty	fabulous	intellectual	powerful	thrilling
brave	fair	intelligent	prepared	thriving
bravo	familiar	inventive	pretty	tops
brilliant	famous	J	principled	tranquil
bubbly	fantastic	jovial	productive	transforming
C	favorable	joy	progress	transformative
calm	fetching	jubilant	prominent	trusting
celebrated	fine	K	protected	truthful
certain	fitting	keen	proud	U
champ	flourishing	kind	Q	unreal
champion	fortunate	knowing	quality	unwavering
charming	free	knowledgeable	quick	up
cheery	fresh	L	quiet	upbeat
choice	friendly	laugh	R	upright
classic	fun	legendary	ready	upstanding
classical	funny	light	reassuring	V
clean	G	learned	refined	valued
commend	generous	lively	refreshing	vibrant
composed	genius	lovely	rejoice	victorious
congratulation	genuine	lucid	reliable	victory
constant	giving	lucky	remarkable	vigorous
cool	glamorous	luminous	resounding	virtuous
courageous	glowing	M	respected	vital
creative	good	marvelous	restored	vivacious
cute	gorgeous	masterful	reward	

What does God say about me?

1. I am fearfully and wonderfully made. (Psalm 139:14)
2. I am the apple of His eye. (Psalm 17)
3. I am "His treasured possession." (Deut 7:6)
4. I will help you to speak and teach you what to say (Ex 4:11)
5. I am an encourager (Isaiah 50:4)
6. God has expressed His kindness to me (Eph 2:7)
7. God's power works through me (Eph 3:7)
8. I am a citizen of heaven (Php 3:20)
9. I am a dwelling for the Holy Spirit (Eph 2:22)
10. I am a holy temple (Eph 2:21; 1Co 6:19)
11. I am a light in the world (Mt 5:14)
12. I am a light to others, and can exhibit goodness, righteousness and truth (Eph 5:8-9)
13. I am a member of Christ's Body (1Co 12:27)
14. I am a member of God's household (Eph 2:19)
15. I am a minister of reconciliation (2Co 5:17-20)
16. I am a new creation (2Co 5:17)
17. I am a personal witness of Jesus Christ (Ac 1:8)
18. I am a saint (Eph 1:18)
19. I am adopted as his child (Eph 1:5)
20. I am alive with Christ (Eph 2:5)
21. I am assured all things work together for good (Ro 8:28)
22. I am blameless (ICo 1:8)
23. I am blessed in the heavenly realms with every spiritual blessing (Eph 1:3)
24. I am born again (IPe 1:23)
25. I am born of God and the evil one cannot touch me (1Jn 5:18)
26. I am chosen and dearly loved (Col3:12)
27. I am chosen before the creation of the world (Eph 1:4, 11)
28. I am Christ's friend (Jn 15:15)
29. I am completed by God (Eph 3:19)
30. I am confident that God will perfect the work He has begun in me (Php 1:6)
31. I am crucified with Christ (Gal 2:20)
32. I am dead to sin (Ro 1:12)
33. I am delivered (Col1:13)
34. I am faithful (Eph 1:1)
35. I am forgiven (Eph 1:8; Col1:14)
36. I am given God's glorious grace lavishly and without restriction (Eph 1:5,8)
37. I am God's child (Jn 1:12)
38. I am God's coworker (2Co 6:1)
39. I am God's workmanship (Eph 2:10)
40. I am growing (Col 2:7)
41. I am healed from sin (IPe 2:24)
42. I am hidden with Christ in God (Col 3:3)
43. I am His disciple (Jn 13:15)

44	I am holy and blameless (Eph 1:4)
45	I am in Him (Eph 1:7; 1Co 1:30)
46	I am included (Eph 1:13)
47	I am more than a conqueror (Ro 8:37)
48	I am no longer condemned (Ro 8:1, 2)
49	I am not alone (Heb 13:5)
50	I am not helpless (Php 4:13)
51	I am not in want (Php 4:19)
52	I am overcoming (IJn 4:4)
53	I am part of God's kingdom (Rev 1:6)
54	I am persevering (Php 3:14)
55	I am prayed for by Jesus Christ (Jn 17:20-23)
56	I am promised a full life (Jn 10:10)
57	I am promised eternal life (Jn 6:47)
58	I am protected (Jn 10:28)
59	I am qualified to share in His inheritance (Col1:12)
60	I am raised up with Christ (Eph 2:6; Col2:12)
61	I am redeemed from the curse of the Law (Gal 3:13)
62	I am safe (IJn 5:18)
63	I am salt and light of the earth (Mt 5:13-14)
64	I am sealed with the promised Holy Spirit (Eph 1:13)
65	I am seated with Christ in the heavenly realms (Eph 2:6)
66	I am secure (Eph 2:20)
67	I am set free (Ro 8:2; Jn 8:32)
68	I am the righteousness of God (2Co 5:21)
69	I am united with other believers (Jn 17:20-23)
70	I am victorious (1Co 15:57)
71	I am victorious (IJn 5:4)
72	I belong to God (1Co 6:20)
73	I can approach God with freedom and confidence (Eph 3:12)
74	I can be certain of God's truths and the lifestyle which He has called me to (Eph 4:17)
75	I can be humble, gentle, patient and lovingly tolerant of others (Eph 4:2)
76	I can be kind and compassionate to others (Eph 4:32)
77	I can be strong (Eph 6:10)
78	I can bring glory to God (Eph 3:21)
79	I can forgive others (Eph 4:32)
80	I can give thanks for everything (Eph 5:20)
81	I can grasp how wide, long, high and deep Christ's love is (Eph 3:18)
82	I can have a new attitude and a new lifestyle (Eph 4:21-32)
83	I can honor God through marriage (Eph 5:22-33)
84	I can mature spiritually (Eph 4:15)
85	I can parent my children with composure (Eph 6:4)
86	I can stand firm in the day of evil (Eph 6:13)
87	I can understand what God's will is (Eph 5:17)
88	I don't have to always have my own agenda (Eph 5:21)

89	I have access to the Father (Eph 2:18)
90	I have been brought near to God through Christ's blood (Eph 2:13)
91	I have been called (Eph 4:1; 2Ti 1:9)
92	I have been chosen and God desires me to bear fruit (Jn 15:1,5)
93	I have been established, anointed and sealed by God (2Co 1:21-22)
94	I have been justified (Ro 5:1)
95	I have been shown the incomparable riches of God's grace (Eph 2:7)
96	I have God's power (Eph 6:10)
97	I have hope (Eph 1:12)
98	I have not been given a spirit of fear, but of power, love and self-discipline (2Ti 1:7)
99	I have peace (Eph 2:14)
100	I have purpose (Eph 1:9 & 3:11)
101	I have redemption (Eph 1:8)
102	I know there is a purpose for my sufferings (Eph 3:13)
103	I possess the mind of Christ (ICo 2:16)
104	I share in the promise of Christ Jesus (Eph 3:6)
105	My heart and mind is protected with God's peace (Php 4:7)

Citations

Feelings and Emotions Vocabulary Word List. (n.d.). Retrieved March 2, 2016, from http://www.enchantedlearning.com/wordlist/emotions.shtml

Geiger, N. (2010, February 6). *100 Things the Bible Says About Me.* Retrieved March 4, 2016, from http://teachingsundayschool.blogspot.com/2010/02/100-things-bible-says-about-me.html

McGrath, E. (2001, November 1). Recovering from Trauma. Retrieved February 17, 2016, from https://www.psychologytoday.com/articles/200308/recovering-trauma

Positive Words Vocabulary Word List. (n.d.). Retrieved March 2, 2016, from http://www.enchantedlearning.com/wordlist/positivewords.shtml

Shakespearean Insult Kit. (n.d.). Retrieved March 3, 2016, from http://studymacbeth.wikispaces.com/file/view/Shakespearian_Insult_Kit.jpg
This is a long standing item - original source undetermined.

The English Standard Version Bible: Containing the Old and New Testaments with Apocrypha. (2009). New York: Oxford University Press.

www.ingramcontent.com/pod-product-compliance
Lightning Source LLC
Chambersburg PA
CBHW081758100526
44592CB00015B/2476